GOVERNMENTS
of the
WESTERN
HEMISPHERE

SUSAN DUDLEY GOLD

TWENTY-FIRST CENTURY BOOKS
A Division of Henry Holt and Company
New York

Dedicated to my son, Samuel Morrison, whose knowledge of government and politics is truly impressive

Twenty-First Century Books
A Division of Henry Holt and Company, Inc.
115 West 18th Street
New York, NY 10011

Henry Holt® and colophon are trademarks of
Henry Holt and Company, Inc.
Publishers since 1866

Library of Congress Cataloging-in-Publication Data
Gold, Susan Dudley
Governments of the western hemisphere/by Susan Dudley Gold.
p. cm.—(Comparing continents)
Includes bibliographical references and index.
1. Comparative government. 2. America—Politics and government. 3. Indians of North America—Politics and government. 4. Indians of South America—Politics and government.
I. Title. II. Series.
JF51.G58   1997
320.3'09181'2—dc2197-15331

CIP

Photo Credits
Cover photographs: © 1996 Photodisc.
Photograph on page 17: © 1996 Photodisc.
Illustrations on pages 3 (center), 7, 42, 50, and 52: North Wind Picture Archives.
Illustrations on pages 3 (top), 27, 35, 57, 65: Library of Congress.
Photographs on pages 3 (bottom), 16, 61, 69, 74, 76, 80, and 86: UPI/Corbis-Bettmann.
Photograph on page 10: Canapress/Tom Hanson.
Maps on pages 4, 18, 22, 24, 26, 29, 31, 32, 33, 36, 37, 46, 49, and 53
© 1997 Susan D. Gold.

Design, Typesetting, and Layout
Custom Communications

ISBN 0-8050-5602-5
First Edition 1997

Printed in Mexico
All first editions are printed on acid-free paper ∞.
1 3 5 7 9 10 8 6 4 2

CONTENTS

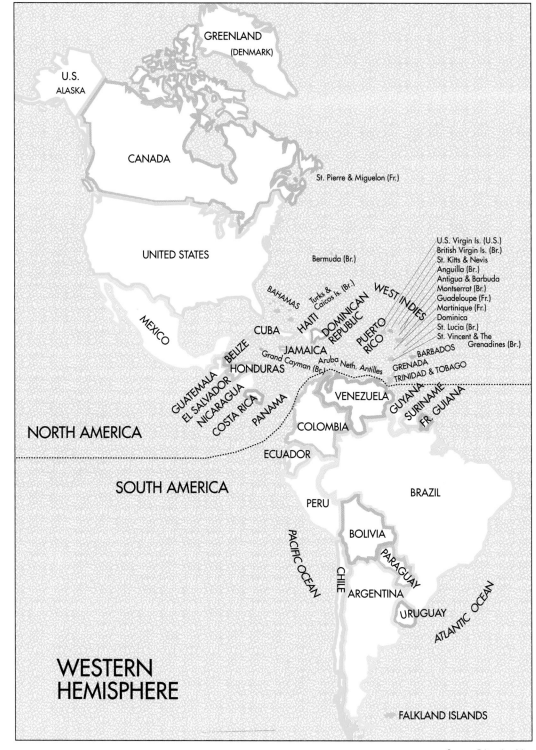

GREENLAND
(DENMARK)

U.S.
ALASKA

CANADA

St. Pierre & Miguelon (Fr.)

UNITED STATES

U.S. Virgin Is. (U.S.)
British Virgin Is. (Br.)
St. Kitts & Nevis
Anguilla (Br.)
Antigua & Barbuda
Montserrat (Br.)
Guadeloupe (Fr.)
Martinique (Fr.)
Dominica
St. Lucia (Br.)
St. Vincent & The
Grenadines (Br.)

Bermuda (Br.)

BAHAMAS

Turks &
Caicos Is. (Br.)

WEST INDIES

MEXICO

CUBA

HAITI

DOMINICAN
REPUBLIC

PUERTO
RICO

JAMAICA
Grand Cayman (Br.)

BELIZE

HONDURAS

GUATEMALA
EL SALVADOR
NICARAGUA
COSTA RICA

PANAMA

Aruba Neth. Antilles

BARBADOS
GRENADA
TRINIDAD & TOBAGO

VENEZUELA

GUYANA
SURINAME
FR. GUIANA

COLOMBIA

NORTH AMERICA

ECUADOR

SOUTH AMERICA

PERU

BRAZIL

BOLIVIA

PACIFIC OCEAN

CHILE

PARAGUAY

ARGENTINA

URUGUAY

ATLANTIC OCEAN

WESTERN
HEMISPHERE

FALKLAND ISLANDS

Source: *Britannica Atlas*

INTRODUCTION

GOVERNING NATIONS

The supreme ruler of the Indians of Peru, the Inca, wore a red-fringed crown, lived in an elaborate palace built especially for him, and had the power to do whatever he wished. When speaking to him, officials hid themselves behind a screen so he would not see them and suddenly order their deaths. The Inca shared power with no one and ruled over an empire covering 350,000 square miles.

George Washington, hero of the American Revolution, reluctantly agreed to serve as the first president of the United States of America. For two terms, he oversaw a form of government that had never been tried before. Using the new Constitution as his guide, Washington forged out his role as elected leader of a free people. He refused to serve a third term, even though he probably would have won reelection. As he left office, Washington warned the young nation against the "baneful effects" of political parties, which he called democracy's "worst enemy."[1]

After the death of her husband, Juan Perón, in

1974, María Estela Martínez de Perón took over the reins of Argentina, the second largest nation in South America. Isabel Perón, as she was known, became the first woman president of a Western Hemisphere nation. Her power, however, came from her name, not her abilities. A former nightclub dancer with a sixth-grade education, she was overthrown by military officers after only twenty-one months in office.

As only the third French Canadian prime minister in Canada's history, Pierre Trudeau firmly opposed French-speaking Quebec's attempts to separate from the rest of the nation. He lost his seat in 1979 when the opposing Progressive Conservative Party gained control of Parliament. But a year later, he won a fourth term as prime minister. Under his leadership, Canada adopted a bill of rights for the nation's citizens and reformed its constitution. The act, signed by Queen Elizabeth II, gave Canada the right to amend its own constitution for the first time.

These leaders of the Western Hemisphere governed their people in very different ways. Each dealt with problems unique to their time and nation. Each filled a particular role as head of the government. And each was influenced by those who had gone before.

Centuries before Christopher Columbus made his fateful journey to the New World, natives in the Western Hemisphere operated under their own forms of government. Some tribes lived in egalitarian societies,

a system where every member had an equal say. Other tribes worshiped a ruler they believed was descended from the sun and who had unlimited power.

When the English came to North America seeking freedom of religion or adventure and riches, they brought with them a tradition of self-government. Noblemen in England, where most of the new settlers originated, had demanded a say in government dating back to the Magna Carta of 1215.

The Spanish and Portuguese conquistadors sailed to the lands of Latin America—Mexico, Central America, and South America—in search of gold. They brought to the New World their languages, religion, and allegiance to kings and queens. Black slaves shipped to the New World from African nations carried with them their own notions of government. Later, immigrants from around the world added their ideas and cultures to the mix.

This patchwork of people and beliefs converged on the two continents of the Western Hemisphere beginning in the early 1500s. By 1830 the populations had divided into independent nations, ruled by individual governments forged from each country's unique blend of cultures. Since then, some nations have seesawed continually between military dictatorships and civilian rule. Others have remained strong, withstanding rebellions and attempted takeovers. Still others have changed gradually, molded by the needs and demands of their people.

WHY GOVERNMENT?

Imagine a world without government. What would happen if your neighbor suddenly decided he wanted to build a garage on your land? What if the local factory stopped treating its waste water in order to save money? Who would decide which parent got custody of the children in a divorce? How would people know which side of the road to drive their cars on or if a food contained an ingredient they shouldn't eat?

No one lives alone in the world. Everyone comes in contact with other people whose actions affect their lives. Government provides the rules that regulate those interactions.

Even small groups of people develop informal systems to put order into their everyday life. A club may adopt a set of rules to determine how decisions will be made. A mother and father may set down rules that their children are expected to follow.

The government of a region determines what is acceptable behavior and what will happen to those who break the rules. In some societies the government is closely tied to religion. In others the government and the church are strictly separated. The government may be run by one person or a handful of people who seek to control every action taken by the people in their realm. In other regions the people may control the government. Governments regulate the economy, the court system, and relations with other governments. They create order and a sense of security for their people. Without government, chaos would reign.

CHAPTER ONE

FORMS OF GOVERNMENTS

The two continents of the Western Hemisphere have been ruled by almost every kind of government that exists. Long before the English and other Europeans made their way to North America, many of the native people lived in small groups loosely connected by shared language or customs. When deciding a course of action that affected these groups, the chiefs of the tribes met in a council to discuss their options. Each tribe, however, had its own leader and its own way of doing things.

This form of government is called a confederation. Under a confederation, several independent units (states, tribes, or other group) join together to address matters that concern them all. The confederation can operate only when all its members agree on a course of action. Each unit can make its own laws and cannot be overruled by the confederation.

The world's most powerful confederation is the

At left, Canadian Prime Minister Jean Chretien gestures while responding to a question from a member of the House of Commons during a question-and-answer session in February 1997.

Commonwealth of Nations, made up of Great Britain and the countries that were once part of the British Empire. Canada and several West Indies island nations, including the Bahamas and Grenada, are among the Western Hemisphere nations that belong to the Commonwealth (see chart at left and on page 13 for a complete listing of Western Hemisphere Commonwealth members). The members of the Commonwealth are all independent nations or political units, linked by their ties to England. England's king or queen serves as the symbolic head of the nations in the Commonwealth.

For thousands of years most nations in the world were ruled by monarchs, men and women who usually inherited their positions. These kings and queens had complete power over their subjects. Some monarchs were wise and fair; others were cruel or bumbling. A few rulers, like the Inca in Peru, claimed to be descended from a god or, in the case of the Spanish kings, to have orders from God—a divine right to rule. Today, most monarchs' power is limited by a code of laws; many share power with elected officials. This is known as a limited or constitutional monarchy.

Greenland, the world's largest island located off the eastern coast of Canada, is part of Denmark and operates as a constitutional monarchy under the Danish queen. Greenland's people vote for their own local parliament, which runs the local government. (See chart for other entities under foreign control.)

Beginning with the American Revolution in 1776,

democracy began to take hold in the New World. Democracy is, in the words of Abraham Lincoln, "government of the people, by the people, and for the people." Under a democratic system, voters elect their own leaders, who are expected to represent the people's interests. Citizens living in a democratic society organize political parties representing varying views, debate issues, and vote in free elections.

The two most common forms of democratic government are the parliamentary and the presidential systems. Canada, Great Britain, and other former British colonies operate under the parliamentary form of government. Citizens in these countries elect members of a parliament or legislature, which runs the country. Citizens don't vote directly for the prime minister or premier, who heads the government. The leader of the party that wins the most seats in the Parliament becomes the prime minister.

The United States operates under the presidential system. Its voters elect members of the legislature, known as Congress, and a president, who is independent of Congress. The two branches of government—the executive and the legislative—share power equally with a third branch, the judicial (courts). The United States and most Latin American nations are considered to be democratic republics, where leaders are elected by the people and there is no hereditary ruler.

In democracies, a leader's power is limited by a constitution, a written document that sets down the rules of government and establishes the rights of citi-

FORMS OF GOVERNMENT

South America:
Argentina: Republic
Bolivia: Republic
Brazil: Republic
Chile: Republic
Colombia: Republic
Ecuador: Republic
*Guyana: Republic
Paraguay: Republic
Peru: Republic
Suriname: Republic
Uruguay: Republic
Venezuela: Republic

* Members of Commonwealth of Nations

UNDER FOREIGN CONTROL

Great Britain: Anguilla, Bermuda, British Virgin Islands, Cayman Islands, Falkland Islands, Montserrat, Turks and Caicos Islands.
United States: Puerto Rico (U.S. Commonwealth), U.S. Virgin Islands.
France: French Guiana, Guadeloupe, Martinique, St. Pierre and Miquelon
Netherlands: Aruba, Netherlands Antilles
Denmark: Greenland

Source: CIA 1996 World Fact Book

A Peaceful Transition

George Washington, first U.S. president, feared political parties would tear the nation apart. Before Washington left office, however, he allied himself with the Federalists, the nation's first political party, founded by Alexander Hamilton. The Federalists, who believed in a strong central government, strengthened their grip on power when their candidate, John Adams, won election to the presidency in 1796.

Adams's vice president, Thomas Jefferson, believed that states should have more power than the federal government. He founded the Democratic-Republican party to reflect those views and ran against Adams in the 1800 presidential campaign.

The campaign was a heated one, and for a while it appeared Washington might have been right in opposing the formation of political parties. Under the system of the time, electors chosen by each state voted for two candidates. The person with the majority of votes became president; the second-highest vote-getter became vice president. When the votes were tallied, Jefferson and Aaron Burr each had seventy-three votes. Adams trailed with sixty-five, and Charles C. Pinckney garnered sixty-four.

The tie-vote threw the race into the hands of the House of Representatives. Jefferson won by a six-vote margin. On March 4, 1801, Jefferson, dressed in everyday clothes instead of the fancy ruffles of the past generation, took the oath of office in the new capital he had helped design. The power of the nation passed peacefully from John Adams's Federalists to Jefferson's Democratic-Republicans. For the first time in U.S. history, one political party had transferred power to an opposing party. It marked the beginning of a tradition of nonviolent transfer that would firmly establish the United States as a constitutional democracy.

zens. It outlines the form of the government and how it will work. A constitution defines the role of the federal (national) and state governments and places limits on their power. It provides a blueprint of the court system. It is regarded as the law of the land; all other laws are measured against the constitution to test whether they are valid. Nations with other types of government may also have constitutions, but powerful leaders may sometimes ignore the rules or discard the constitution altogether.

Communism originally meant a system in which property and goods are shared and owned by all. Today's version of communism developed out of the writings of Karl Marx, a German philosopher. He envisioned a classless society in which everyone owned land and property jointly.

In many nations (China, the former Soviet Union), communism developed into totalitarianism. People living in a totalitarian state are ruled strictly by one person or group of persons; the state controls all aspects of their lives. Though the citizens vote, candidates from only one party—the Communist Party—appear on the ballot. The government allows no opposition; speech and the press are muzzled. People are not allowed to practice their religion freely. They are expected to embrace the ideals and beliefs of communism. Most property belongs to the state, which is controlled by the ruling Communists. The individual has few rights and is inferior to the state. Cuba is the only Communist nation in the Western Hemisphere.

Fidel Castro, pictured in 1960, has ruled as dictator over Cuba since 1959. Cuba is currently the only Communist nation in the Western Hemisphere. Other nations have Communist factions and political parties.

Dictatorships are governments run by one person. A dictator may head a totalitarian state or hold communist views. Some dictators believe in the private ownership of property and oppose communism. Other dictators adopt no philosophy at all other than gaining and keeping power for themselves.

Regardless of beliefs, dictators rule with an iron hand, with little or no regard for the rights of their people. All the power of government is centered in the dictator, who is commander of the armed forces as well as head of state. Often, as has been the case in numerous countries in Latin America, dictators have won their positions by force, as head of a rebel group or with the help of the military. When members of the armed forces overthrow a government already in place, it is called a military coup.

Dictatorships are among the most unstable types of government. Constitutions and laws remain in effect only if they coincide with the dictator's views. Courts have no power to overrule the dictator's actions. There are no permanent rules. People living under a dictator may adore their leader, but they have no peaceable way to challenge actions they don't like. Opponents must resort to force to topple the regime, and they often do. Their attempts to unseat the ruler—successful or not—result in turmoil. In a few cases, as in Cuba where Fidel Castro has ruled as a dictator since 1959, dictators manage to hold power for years.

CHAPTER TWO

NATIVE RULE

O n October 12, 1492, Christopher Columbus, the Italian sailor financed by Spain,
set foot on the lands of the Western
Hemisphere. He thought he had discov-
ered a new passage to the East Indies and called the
natives there Indians. Columbus's discovery of a new
world would have a devastating effect on these early
civilizations of the Western Hemisphere.

MAYANS

The Mayans in Mexico, Guatemala, and Belize
(formerly called British Honduras) had perhaps the
most sophisticated civilization among Western Hemisphere natives. During the height of their civilization,
from about A.D. 300 to 900, the Mayans developed an
intricate calendar, a complex system of writing with
symbols called hieroglyphics, and elaborate temples
and pyramids. They knew mathematics and astronomy
at a level rivaling European scientists of the time.

Members of the royal family ruled the Mayans.

*Above, the
ruins of
Mayan temples
built centuries
before Colum-
bus discovered
the New World.*

Priests and soldiers were also part of the ruling class. Around A.D. 900, the nobles rebelled and killed the Mayan ruler. As warfare engulfed their world, the farmers built walls around their homes to protect themselves. Eventually, with crops destroyed and trade disrupted by the wars, the people dispersed into small settlements where they lived off the land as best they could. Others retreated to Mexico's Yucatan section to the north, where they set up a new civilization that flourished until the thirteenth century. That, too, disintegrated as civil war erupted.

By the time the Spaniards landed in 1517, the Mayans had abandoned their spectacular cities and lived in small bands. The Aztecs had assumed power over the Mexican lands. An epidemic brought to the New World by the Spaniards killed many of the remaining Mayans. Those surviving were enslaved by their European captors or went into hiding in the wild lands of Mexico and Central America. Many of their ancestors live there today.

AZTECS

Hernán Cortes and his band of adventurers must have been amazed when, in 1519, they reached the Aztec capital city of Tenochtitlán. Centered on an island in the Valley of Mexico, the Aztec capital was a bustling metropolis with paved streets, huge markets, and a population the size of the largest Spanish city. A stupefying array of palaces, temples, public buildings,

Source: *Latin America: A General History*

and luxurious homes filled the central square. Pyramids, their steps gleaming, awaited human sacrifices. A series of causeways and bridges connected the main city to nearby islands.

Aztec ruler Montezuma II, unsure whether the Spaniards were gods or enemies, greeted them cautiously. The Aztec monarch ruled over an uneasy empire that stretched from the Gulf of Mexico to the Pacific and covered most of central and southern Mexico. By the time the Spaniards entered their domain, the Aztecs controlled many conquered tribes, including the Chichimecs, the Toltecs, the Zapotecs, and what remained of the Maya tribes. The rebellious tribes were kept under control only through force. Many were killed as sacrifices to the nation's gods.

The Aztecs did not believe their ruler was a god, but they treated him like a king, supplying him with palaces, extensive gardens, and whatever he desired. Montezuma had zoos filled with exotic animals and two thousand servants to wait on him. A council made up of one hundred military men, religious leaders, and high-ranking officials chose the Aztec leader from the members of the royal family. Though he acted as supreme ruler of the Aztecs, the emperor accepted advice from the council. He also received help from a second-in-command, who oversaw routine matters.[1]

The chiefs of the twenty Aztec tribes supervised the people in their villages and gave the emperor advice on war and other important matters. Each tribe was divided into clans called *calpullis*. The clan controlled

The Return of the Bearded God

Weeks before the Spaniards arrived in the Aztec capital of Tenochtitlán, spies had sent Montezuma pictures they had drawn of Hernán Cortes's armored men, his awe-inspiring ships, and his fearsome guns. Montezuma, a weak leader who relied on superstition, believed Cortes was a god who would punish his people.

Cortes, who had conquered several neighboring tribes and won them over as allies, learned from the Aztec's neighbors the story of Quetzalcoatl, a serpent god with feathers, who was thought to have once been a wise king exiled from his realm in the lands of the Aztecs. The king had pledged to return and reclaim his kingdom.

In one account, Quetzalcoatl was described as a bearded white man (like the bearded Cortes); some say he may have been a European who had found his way to the New World in earlier times.

Montezuma sent a message asking Cortes to leave and offered gifts to appease him. With perfect timing, Cortes arrived in Tenochtitlán on the day the Aztecs celebrated as Quetzalcoatl's birthday. Thousands of Aztecs stood aside as he and his men marched unharmed into their capital. Montezuma, carried on a litter covered with jewels, greeted the Spanish conquistador as if he were supernatural. Cortes told the Aztec emperor he had been sent by a great ruler across the sea. But Montezuma, fearing the worst, believed the bearded king had returned to earth.

Latin America: A General History

the land; the clan leaders saw to it that their people farmed it. The leaders, who came from the upper classes of Aztec society, inherited their posts. On the local level they were supreme, supervising practically everything clan members did. During wars, clan leaders led their people into battle.[2]

Aztec laws were harsh, though they guaranteed certain rights even to slaves. Members of the upper class elected judges to serve in the people's court. Defendants found guilty of murder or theft received a death sentence. Those convicted of spreading malicious rumors had their lips cut off.[3]

Captives from conquered tribes paid heavily for their defeat. The Aztecs sacrificed thousands of them to their gods, brutally murdering them atop the steps of the pyramids. Montezuma also required the defeated tribe members to pay tribute to him in the form of gold, jade, and other prized possessions.

The emperor failed, however, to set up a government to rule over the captive tribes or to involve them in Aztec society. Whenever they rebelled, Montezuma sent warriors to subdue them. The resentful tribes eventually joined forces with Cortes and his men to overthrow their hated captors.

INCAS

The Incas ruled over a colossal region that once stretched for 350,000 square miles through Peru, Ecuador, Chile, and Argentina, and from the Amazon

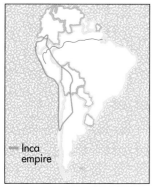

Inca
empire

Source: *Latin America:
A General History*

jungles to the Pacific Ocean. The Inca kingdom was the most efficient and highly organized civilization in the Western Hemisphere.

Unlike the Aztecs the Incas involved defeated tribes in their society. Everyone within the Inca realm was required to speak a universal language, Quechua. The language is still spoken today in large parts of South America. To strengthen the bonds further, the Incas adopted many of the conquered tribes' pagan gods, festivals, and rituals. They also developed an extensive road system and used couriers to connect villages and towns within the Inca borders. Defeated tribes refusing to adopt the Incan language and customs were divided into small groups and driven away.

All power centered around the ruler, known as the Inca, who was thought to be a direct descendant of the sun god. The Inca inherited the top post from his father who, under Inca rule, mated with his sister to produce the next royal leader. He controlled the empire's government, religion, and social life. The Inca shared command with no one; all orders had to be approved by him.

Serving under the Inca were nobles and priests. Lower officials kept the population under control. The four highest officials lived in Cuzco, the Inca capital, and each supervised one-quarter of the kingdom. Each province had its own leader, or governor, a nobleman who usually inherited the post from his father. On the local level, chieftains oversaw the government. The most powerful chiefs were in charge of ten thousand adult males. (Women and children, who had no political power, were not included in the count.) Other chiefs supervised groups of five thousand, one thousand, five hundred, or one hundred adult men, depending on their importance. Foremen, who took their orders from the chiefs, oversaw ten to fifty people in their areas.[4]

The entire system was based on a rigid chain of command, with the Inca giving orders at the top. Loyalty and spies kept everyone in line. The members of the nobility were the strongest defenders of the system, which guaranteed them prestige and positions in government.

When Spanish conquistador Francisco Pizarro arrived in Peru in 1532, he found a glorious empire, with magnificent palaces, gold, and jewels everywhere. But it was also an empire weakened by the recent rift between the Inca's sons. The Spaniards, eager to claim the Incas' gold, made good use of their guns, military tactics, and horses. Though vastly outnumbered by the Incas, Pizarro and 184 men managed to capture the head Inca. Because all power revolved around the Inca, once he was captured, the Inca forces had no one to direct them and the empire collapsed. The Spaniards claimed the land.

THE WANDERERS

Several other tribes lived in the wilds of Central and South America. Banding together in small groups that wandered through jungles and mountains, the tribes were able to escape from the Incas, and later, the Spaniards. Among them were the Araucanians of southern Chile, the Guaraní of Paraguay, and the Aymará in Bolivia. The Arawak and the Carib lived in the Amazon basin, while the Chibcha ruled in Colombia. The ancestors of many of these native tribes still live in Latin America today.

Life for these tribes was simple. They spent most of their days gathering nuts and berries, hunting, and fishing. Clans, or groups of related families, lived in small groups, with elder tribe members—usuaily men but sometimes women— serving as leaders. Rituals, customs, and family traditions spelled out the role of each member of the society. Most of these tribes were too small to have a formal governmental structure.

NORTH AMERICAN NOMADS, FARMERS, AND WARRIORS

Like their counterparts to the south, many of the native tribes in North America were nomads who moved from place to place searching for food. Even those who planted gardens often moved to other areas in winter or when crops would no longer grow in the depleted soil. The nomads had little time or energy to develop intricate political structures.

These tribes lived informally, usually in clusters based on families. The oldest male generally acted as leader of the group, although in some tribes women played a major role. They led peaceful lives and rarely

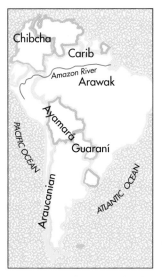

Source: *Latin America: A General History*

came into contact with anyone who was not related. The occasional fight was settled quickly among the parties involved.

The governments of farming tribes with extensive gardens and villages often were controlled by those who had possessions. Those who owned the most blankets, the best canoes, or the largest crew of slaves (captured from other tribes) had positions of power in the tribe. Though disagreements between tribe members frequently led to fights, foes also settled disputes by paying off their enemies.[5]

Those who owned horses, brought to the New World by the Europeans, had more to protect from their enemies than those who wandered on foot. Their governments focused on war, often led by skilled warriors. In the Northwest plains young men joined warrior societies, where they learned to fight, and proved themselves by stealing horses, killing enemies, or performing brave deeds in battle. Positions of power went to the best warriors, prophets who had visions, and those who owned the most horses.[6]

THE IROQUOIS LEAGUE

Some Native Americans in North America joined together in loose associations known as confederations. Perhaps the most successful of these was the Iroquois League or Confederation. This group, believed to have been formed in the mid-1500s, united five Indian tribes—the Senecas, Cayugas, Onondagas, Onei-

Source: *Shepherd's Historical Atlas*

das, and Mohawks. All shared the Iroquois language. At the beginning of the 1700s, the Tuscarora tribe joined the confederation. English-speaking colonists labeled the league the Five Nations, and later, the Six Nations. Some believe the confederation—with its code of laws and representational government— served as a guide for the American revolutionists when they devised the U.S. Constitution.

The Indians in this vast network lived in New York, from Lake Ontario and the Adirondack Mountains in the north to the Catskill Mountains in the south. At one time, the mighty confederation occupied land as far west as the Mississippi River.

Each tribe retained its independence and identity within the larger confederation. The Great Council Fire, the governing body of the league, was made up of fifty representatives from the tribes. The Onondaga had the most members, fourteen in all. The Cayuga was represented by ten council members; the Mohawk and the Oneida by nine apiece, and the Seneca by eight. Council members were men, selected by the head woman in each clan. They served for life and met yearly to discuss strategies and plan the confederation's activities.

Despite the unequal number of representatives on the council, the tribes had equal say in the league. Major actions required a unanimous vote of approval by the council. Council members who misbehaved or were not properly representing their tribe could be impeached, or removed from office.

Tee Yee Neen Ho Ga Row, emperor of the Six Nations, a confederation of Iroquois tribes in the Northeast

Within each tribe, government followed a similar pattern. Tribe members lived in villages occupied by their mother's relatives. Each village had a council, made up of the wise elders of the tribe. Often, the wisest or most able person was chosen as chief; sometimes the position was inherited. Before making important decisions, the chief consulted with the council. Younger men and women, too, were often included in the discussion. Chiefs rarely made decisions on their own.

William Penn, the founder of Pennsylvania, who tried to treat his Iroquois neighbors fairly, was impressed by their way of governing. In a letter to the Free Society of Traders in London in 1683, he wrote: "Nothing of moment is undertaken, be it war, peace, selling of land, or traffic, without advising with them [old and wise men of the tribe]; and, which is more, with the young men, too. It is admirable to consider how powerful the Kings are, and yet how they move by the breath of their people."[7]

The tribes first formed the Iroquois League to ensure peace among themselves and to protect the individual tribes against a common enemy: the Huron tribe and its allies, who threatened war. The strategy worked; the size and strength of the confederation served to deter enemies and keep the peace. Later, the members of the confederation used their power to negotiate deals with the European settlers who wanted their lands. They offered their services to the British during conflicts with the French in return for protection and manufactured goods. Later, they fought against the Americans in the Revolutionary War. With the British defeat, the league lost its strongest ally. The frenzied land grab that followed broke the back of the confederation.

In 1788 the Iroquois joined with seven other tribes in a huge confederation aimed at protecting Indian land from American settlers. The members promised not to sell land unless every tribe in the confederation had first agreed to the sale. In some cases, though, tribes decided to give the settlers what they wanted in order to keep the peace. But their concessions did not work for long; a new wave of settlers appeared, demanding more land.

The quest for land by settlers and speculators did

more than rob the tribes of their property. It also corrupted their governments and way of life. Land speculators bribed chiefs with trinkets and rum, then convinced the drunken leaders to sign treaties for their tribes. The chiefs had no authority to give away the tribes' land, but the speculators used the treaties to get what they wanted anyway. Though many chiefs resisted the temptations, others—corrupted by greed and alcohol—sold out their people. Members of the tribes could no longer depend on their chiefs to represent their interests.

THE INUIT WAY

The Inuit live in the northern reaches of the Western Hemisphere, in a vast stretch of land from Greenland to northeast Siberia. Inuit means "real people" in the native language. Native Americans to the south labeled them Eskimo, a term picked up by the European settlers.[9]

Because the harsh northern terrain could not support large numbers of people, the Inuit lived in small family groups. Inuit parents usually lived with their children and their married sons and their families in an egalitarian society where everyone had an equal say. Their daughters went to live with their husband's families when they wed. Families banded together to harvest the fish and other game in their frigid homelands.

The group's members lived by rules set by their ancestors that limited who they could marry, who inher-

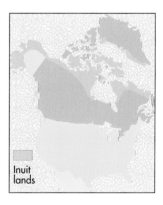

Inuit lands

Source: *People of the Ice and Snow*

PUNISHING AN OFFENDER INUIT STYLE

The Inuits use ridicule to punish someone who has committed a minor crime or offense. Members of the group sing a song known as the drum-dance song that makes fun of the offender. They also laugh derisively at the guilty one. Once offenders mend their ways and stop the bad behavior, the songs are ended and the misdemeanors forgotten.

This helps to keep resentments from building among the Inuit, who depend on each other to survive in the harsh conditions of the Arctic.

People of the Deer by Farley Mowat

ited rights to property, and how people should act. The oldest man in the group was considered the leader, as long as he was still able to hunt. He settled disputes and handled relations with outside groups.

Because of their far northern location, the Inuit had little contact with Europeans until the early 1700s. Vitus Bering, a Danish captain serving Russian Czar Peter the Great, landed on Alaskan soil in 1741 and claimed the area for Russia. After his crew returned to Russia with pelts from sea otters and seals, Russian adventurers soon headed for Alaska to make their fortunes. In the northeast, European adventurers and crews aboard whaling boats introduced the Inuit to guns and whiskey. Both contributed to the downfall of the Inuit's traditional way of life.

CHAPTER THREE

COLONIAL PERIOD

As word of Christopher Columbus's discovery of land reached Europe, France and England hurriedly made plans to send their own expeditions west. In 1497 John Cabot was hired by Henry VII to find a quicker route to the East Indies. Instead, the Italian-born sailor discovered Newfoundland; a later explorer, Sir Humphrey Gilbert, staked a claim to the land for England. Sebastian Cabot, John Cabot's son, sailed to the New World in 1508 and discovered Hudson Bay. Farther south, English settlers established Jamestown in Virginia in 1607 and Plymouth in Massachusetts in 1620.

French explorers searching for gold under the leadership of Jacques Cartier landed on Gaspé Peninsula in Quebec in 1534. The following year, Cartier and his expedition sailed up the St. Lawrence River to Montreal. In 1541 the French established a settlement there, but it collapsed after two years. French explorer

Source: *Compton's Encyclopedia*

Source: *Compton's Encyclopedia*

Samuel de Champlain founded Quebec in 1608. Other French explorers claimed land in Newfoundland for the crown.

It wasn't long before British and French forces clashed over the land they both claimed in North America. In 1613 Englishmen burned the French settlement at Port Royal in Nova Scotia, Canada. The French later reclaimed the area. But after a disastrous war with England, the French lost Nova Scotia and Newfoundland to England in the Treaty of Utrecht in 1713. In 1755 and 1758 the English would force the entire French community of six thousand to leave Nova Scotia. The French Acadians, as they were called, set up a new life in New Orleans.

Throughout the 1600s and into the 1700s, the French and English battled each other for control of North America. The native tribes, caught between two warring factions, sided with the group that offered them the best deal. They lost regardless. The tribes' English allies stole their land; their French allies failed to protect them from attack.

At the end of the French and Indian War (called the Seven Years' War in Europe) in 1763, the French lost all claim to lands in America. Under Napoleon Bonaparte, the nation reclaimed lands west of the Mississippi but later sold the entire parcel to the United States as the Louisiana Purchase. The French influence remained in a few French strongholds like New Orleans in the United States and Quebec in Canada. But for the most part, the governments of North

America were fashioned by the British and their American and Canadian descendants.

Spain and Portugal quickly established claim to the lands in Central and South America. Portuguese sailor Pedro Álvares Cabral discovered Brazil in 1500 and claimed the region for his homeland. In 1511 Hernán Cortes helped conquer Cuba for Spain, then took his own force to Mexico, where he defeated the Aztecs and other tribes. In 1532 Francisco Pizarro added the huge Incan empire, stretching over Peru, Ecuador, Chile, and Argentina, to the Spanish realm.

The decline of the native populations made it obvious that a new breed of leaders would rule over the lands of the Western Hemisphere. The Europeans (mostly Spanish and Portuguese) in South and Central America and the Europeans (mostly English) in North America would choose very different ways in which to govern their new lands. To understand why, let's look at the Europe of the sixteenth and seventeenth centuries. The events there had a strong influence on the leaders of the New World.

The English government underwent major changes during this time. By the mid-1600s, a growing middle class began to take over power in Parliament. They gained so much strength that in 1649 a group of Puritans headed by Oliver Cromwell beheaded the king and took over the government. Though the monarchy was reinstated in 1660, it never regained absolute power. The true seat of power rested—and still rests—in the Parliament. In 1688 King William and

Mexico, Cuba claimed for Spain by Cortes

Inca lands claimed for Spain by Pizarro

Brazil claimed for Portugal by Cabral

Source: *Latin America: A General History*

After two failed expeditions to find the Incas, Francisco Pizarro drew a line in the sand and dared the men who were courageous enough to join him in one more venture to cross the line. Twelve men met Pizarro's challenge.

Queen Mary, serving as joint monarchs, signed the Declaration of Rights, upon which the U.S. Bill of Rights was later based. The Church of England became the official religion.

In Spain and Portugal kings and queens continued to rule with an iron hand. Their people had little say in government. The monarchs ruled by divine right, responsible only to God. Threatened by the Reformation in other parts of Europe, the Roman Catholic Church became more conservative and allied itself more closely with the reigning monarchs in Spain and Portugal. The Roman Catholic Church upheld the monarch's right to rule and, in turn, controlled the spiritual life of the people.

These two differing styles of government carried over into the New World. The English, crowded off the land on their tiny island nation, sailed to the New World to find a place to build homes. Already with a taste of self-government, they expected to take control of their new homeland. Other European settlers in North America were seeking a land where they could have freedom to worship as they chose.

The Spanish and Portuguese came to the New World for far different reasons. Most of the early explorers wanted to find gold and silver. They had no intention of settling in the new lands.

NORTH AMERICAN COLONIES

Again, world events influenced the future of the

The Spanish and Portuguese monarchs considered their New World lands to be their own personal property.

New World settlements. England defeated Spain, then France as ruler of the sea. With little time or inclination to micromanage affairs in the untamed New World, England centered its attention on expanding its empire in India, Africa, and other parts of the world.

The North American colonists set up the first representative government in the New World in 1619 in Virginia. This House of Burgesses (citizens) had twenty-two members who voted on local laws. A year later, a group of English Pilgrims, far off course, landed in Massachusetts. Since they were outside the rule of the charter established for Virginia, where they had intended to land, the new settlers drew up their own charter. In the pact, called the Mayflower Compact,

Above, the English Pilgrims signed the Mayflower Compact in 1620 that outlined the rules of government for their new colony.

the men pledged to join together to enact "just & equall lawes" for the good of the colony.[1]

Other colonists soon followed suit. In 1649 Maryland settlers passed a law allowing citizens the freedom to worship as they pleased. As settlements grew into towns, colonists set up local governments to establish the rights and duties of citizens and to handle local disputes and pass local laws. The men elected representatives to serve in assemblies, which helped govern each colony. Left on their own, the new Americans had little desire to break away from England. They still regarded England as the mother country, which helped protect their colonies from being overrun by French settlers and Indians.

In the northern part of the continent, almost sixty thousand French settlers remained on land now ruled by their historic enemy. Many of them lived in the province of Quebec. Though they shared the colony, the French and English settlers had different languages, religions, and cultures. While the French had to live under a criminal justice system set up by the English, they still used their own laws in civil cases. The Quebec Act of 1774 made both systems the law of the land. The merging—and friction—of these two cultures would continue throughout Canada's history as a colony, and later, as an independent nation.

LATIN AMERICAN COLONIES

The experience of European settlers in Central

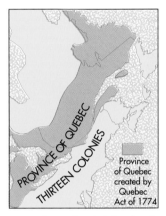

PROVINCE OF QUEBEC

THIRTEEN COLONIES

Province of Quebec created by Quebec Act of 1774

Source: *Compton's Encyclopedia*

and South America was far different. With the defeat of the Spanish Armada in 1588 by the English and the loss of its colonies in India, Spain began to focus on its Western Hemisphere empire.

The Spanish king, who considered the land in the New World his personal property, set up an elaborate system to ensure his control over the government. He divided the Spanish territory into four sections, called viceroyalties. Mexico City served as the capital of New Spain, which included Mexico and stretched from New Mexico to Guatemala. New Granada, with its capital at Bogotá, occupied the northwest corner of South America, in the present-day countries of Colombia, Panama, Ecuador, and Venezuela. Most of the vast holdings of the Incas were ruled by the viceroyalty of Peru. Its capital was Lima. Rio de la Plata, the fourth viceroyalty, covered Argentina, Bolivia, Paraguay, and Uruguay with Buenos Aires as capital.

Viceroys served as the king's representative in each viceroyalty. They lived in fancy palaces, commanded the army, ruled over lower officials, and enforced the laws.

In 1524 the king established the Royal and Supreme Council of the Indies. The council, based in Spain and composed of high Spanish officials, made the laws under which the citizens of Spain's New World empire were expected to live. By 1624 the Council had passed almost 500,000 laws regulating everything from church duties to taxes to everyday behavior in the New World.[2] The Council also exerted control over the

Source: *Latin America: A General History*

viceroys and made sure they were loyal to the king. At the end of each viceroy's term, which usually lasted about three years, he had to report to the Council and answer any charges against him.

Captains-general oversaw less important regions, such as Guatemala, Cuba, and Chile. Governors, appointed in Spain, ruled under the viceroy and captains-general. Then came mayors, who served under the governors.

Each local area had a military chief, who could issue orders to the citizens and who acted as local judge. Officials called *corregidors* ruled each town and oversaw the villages where the native tribes lived. In areas where the viceroy had little interest, local officials ruled like mini-kings over their segment of the New World empire.[3]

The court system followed the Spanish code of justice. First established in the New World in 1511, the high court, or *audiencia,* had branches in each major territory. The audiencia's decisions were final in all but the most important cases. Those went to the Council for a hearing.

The king also appointed religious leaders to their posts in the church. As in Spain, the leaders of the church supported the government's rule.

Almost all the officials, from the viceroy on down, were born in Spain. Officials were known as *peninsulares,* meaning people from the Iberian Peninsula, where Spain and Portugal are located. To ensure that officials retained their strong bonds to Spain, they

THE LIFE OF A VICEROY

As the king's representative, the viceroy lived like royalty in the New World. The family's palace, attended by guards in elegant uniforms, provided all the luxuries of the day.

In eighteenth century Peru, the new viceroy was greeted with great pomp as he arrived from Spain. Officials draped a ceremonial sash around his neck on the outskirts of the capital city of Lima. Then the new viceroy, accompanied by officials clad in their fanciest robes, paraded into town. All along the route, elegant tapestries hung from doorways, and thousands cheered and waved banners. At the cathedral, the archbishop conducted an elaborate reception for the new official. The celebration lasted for twelve days. It was a good show.

Most of the viceroy's days were filled with the mundane duties that come with running a bureaucracy. He listened to merchants' complaints, resolved arguments, and oversaw the economy. The viceroy had the power to interfere in trials, but he seldom did. He was the highest official in Spanish America, but his power was brief, usually only three or four years.

The job wasn't always easy. The Marquis of Leyva, who served as viceroy of New Spain in the mid-1600s, had to cope with the eruption of a volcano, a duel involving a prominent family's son, and an Indian revolt. Perhaps his most trying moment came when the local people staged a violent rally protesting the viceroy's wife's attempts to change the route of a religious parade. She had wanted to be able to see the procession from the palace.

Latin America: A General History

were banned from running a business in the New World or from marrying. They were expected to return to Spain when their tour of duty was over, although many stayed in America.

The common people had little say in the government at any level. Even the rich landowners, the sons of the conquistadors who had been born in America, had little control over political matters. Known as creoles, these American-born Spaniards elected their fellow landowners to seats on the town council, or *cabilda*. These leaders regulated market conditions and set prices, acted as courts for local disputes, and took care of other municipal matters. They had no real power, however, since all their actions had to be approved by the king's corregidors.

In Brazil the Portuguese set up a viceroyalty similar to those in Spanish America. Portugal's Council set the laws for the country's colony; its officials saw to it that the citizens obeyed.

By the beginning of the eighteenth century, Latin America was divided into two ruling groups. Creoles owned the land, while the peninsulares controlled the power. In both Spanish America and Brazil, the government system was filled with corrupt officials. Without official power, the creoles used their wealth to bribe officials to grant them favors or appoint them to town offices.

Despite the corruption and the strict rule, however, there were few rebellions during this time. Black slaves, who had been brought to Latin America in the

1500s, and Indians had no reason to favor the creoles over the Spanish king. The king and the church tried to protect the Indians and blacks from being abused by the creoles, who owned the mines and the farms where they worked.

The creoles were free to practice their Roman Catholic religion, which was also the religion of the state. Although they wanted more say in the government, they still considered themselves Spanish. Their families had always lived under a powerful monarch; it was their way of life. Royal birthdays, coronations, and marriages were celebrated with as much excitement in the New World as in Spain.[4]

The creoles wanted reforms, but they feared revolution. They watched nervously as the blacks in Haiti overthrew their French oppressors and the French masses in Paris beheaded their king during the French Revolution. These rich landowners didn't want to lose power to the Indians, blacks, and mestizos (Latin Americans of Spanish and Indian ancestry). Only when the Spanish and Portuguese kings lost power would the creoles seek to establish a government of their own.

In the 1780s, José Gabriel Condorcanqui Noguera, a mestizo who took the name Tupac Amaru II after an Inca leader, led a rebellion among Indians in Peru and neighboring regions. The rebels attacked people of mixed races as well as Spaniards. Spanish forces crushed the revolt and executed its leader, who had claimed to be descended from Inca royalty.

CHAPTER FOUR

SEEKING INDEPENDENCE

For two-and-one-half centuries after Columbus made his momentous discovery, adventurers from England, France, Spain, Portugal, and other nations carved out a new life in the lands of the Western Hemisphere. But just as the European quest for land and riches forever disrupted the lives of the natives in the New World, so the events in Europe would change the destiny of these new inhabitants.

A war would sharply reduce France's hold on North America. A haughty English king would try to reassert power over British colonies. And the monarchs of Spain and Portugal would lose their thrones. The shift in power would have the effect of an earthquake in the New World.

At left, Antonio José Sucre led his army to victory against Spanish forces high in the Andes in December 1824. The battle marked the end of Spanish control over South America.

Until 1763, when the French and Indian War ended, the colonists in English-speaking North America had fairly good relations with England. British soldiers had helped the colonists drive the French from their lands and quell the Indian uprisings. Trade with England brought riches to American merchants.

Trouble between the two lands began with the rule of King George III. A stubborn man who wanted more power, he was eager to show the colonists that he was in charge. With the help of King George's friends in Parliament, England began imposing new taxes on the Americans. In 1764 Parliament passed the Sugar Act. It raised duties on sugar and increased the list of products that were taxed.

The colonists were outraged. England, they said, had no right to tax them. They would pay taxes only to their own governments. Some British leaders urged the king to reach an agreement with the Americans. He refused.

In 1765 Parliament passed two more laws that infuriated the colonists. One forced the Americans to put up British soldiers in their homes. The second, the Stamp Act, required the colonists to pay taxes on newspapers and business documents. Enraged at these laws, leaders in nine of the thirteen colonies met in New York to protest the new taxes. They declared their right as British citizens not to be taxed by a government in which they had no representatives. Throughout the American colonies, people met in secret societies known as the Sons of Liberty. These groups led the call to separate the colonies from England. Pamphlets, newspapers, and circulars spread their revolutionary ideas to readers throughout the region.

Parliament repealed the Stamp Act the following year, but other taxes soon followed. Tensions exploded when colonists, angered over a new tax on tea, dumped boxes of tea into Boston Harbor in December 1773. The protest led England to impose severe laws on the unruly colonists. These new laws closed Boston Harbor and sharply cut the powers of the Massachusetts assembly, among other things.

This was too much for the independent colonists. For years, they had managed their own affairs. The only way to win back control, they believed, was to go to war against England.

On July 2, 1776, colonial leaders voted to seek independence. Two days later, they signed the Declaration of Independence. The war that followed pitted well-trained British troops against ragtag armies of colonial volunteers. But the Americans knew the terrain, adopted techniques they had learned from Indian warriors, and fought with a passion reserved for those who are defending their homeland. With help from the French, who entered the war in 1778 against their old enemy, the colonists won their freedom. In 1781 Lord Cornwallis surrendered to General George Washington after American and French soldiers defeated the British army at Yorktown, Virginia. The

Treaty of Paris, signed in 1783, officially ended the American Revolution.

CANADIAN INDEPENDENCE

Almost 40,000 American settlers loyal to England fled north to Canada during and after the Revolutionary War. These new immigrants put pressure on the French residents in eastern Canada struggling to retain their way of life.

As colonies of Great Britain, the lands of Canada were part of a limited monarchy headed by King George III. After England's defeat in the American Revolution, moderate forces in the English Parliament regained power under the leadership of William Pitt. Like their British counterparts, Canadian citizens decided most local issues through representatives serving on provincial parliaments. The English Parliament suspended many of the irksome laws imposed on Canada by King George before the Revolutionary War.

In 1791 the province of Quebec was split into two colonies: Lower Canada (east) and Upper Canada (west). Lower Canada, which later became Quebec, was home for many of the French colonists whose forebears had settled in eastern Canada and the northeastern United States, in the area known as New France.

Upper Canada, today known as Ontario, became the center of the English-speaking population. Both new colonies had their own elected assemblies. Nova Scotia, Prince Edward Island, and New Brunswick also

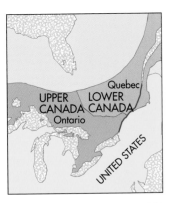

Source: *Confederation 1867: The Creation of the Dominion of Canada*

had assemblies of their own. A governor appointed by the king and his executive council headed the government of each colony. Newfoundland and the lands to the west—outposts with few European settlers—would not elect representatives until the next century.

During the War of 1812, the United States invaded the Canadian colonies, but the British turned back most of the attacks. The Treaty of Ghent that ended the war left things almost as they had been before the war. England's defense of Canada against the United States helped strengthen the bonds between the northern colonies and their mother country.

Friction erupted in Lower Canada when the elected assembly, controlled by French Canadians, tried to override rulings by the English executive council. Frustrated in their attempts, the French Canadians, led by Louis Joseph Papineau, rebelled in November 1837. In Upper Canada another group of French Canadians led by William Lyon Mackenzie joined the battle. English and Canadian troops quickly crushed both revolts. The hostility between French and English Canadians, however, continued to simmer.

The English, who had perhaps learned a lesson after losing their colonies to the south, responded to the troubles by sending the Earl of Durham to Canada. The Earl recommended joining Upper and Lower Canada and putting the elected assemblies in charge of the colonial governments. Both changes were made. By 1855 Canadian colonies had achieved the right to govern their own affairs.

Quebec's Fight For Independence

Quebec, Canada's only French-dominated province, has always sought control over its society. The Quebec Act of 1774, the British North America Act of 1867, and other laws granted Quebec the right to retain the French language and civil procedures.

Many French-speaking Quebec citizens, however, pushed for more power for their province and less control by the federal government. In 1980 a referendum that called for Quebec's independence lost by a 20 percent margin. Undeterred, separatists led the fight against the Canada Act of 1982 because the new reforms did not include more power for Quebec. The act went into effect anyway, without Quebec's support. An amendment to the Act forged at Meech Lake in 1987 would have granted Quebec special status as a "distinct society." But the other provinces refused to give the proposal their support and it failed.

Frustrated in their attempts to win protection for their unique culture, Quebec separatists sponsored another referendum. In February 1996 Quebec voted to remain Canadian by a margin of less than 1 percent. Quebec Premier Jacques Parizeau pledged to continue the fight for independence. "We want a country," he said, "and we shall have it." *USA Today*

For the next several years, each of Canada's five colonies—Prince Edward Island, Nova Scotia, New Brunswick, Newfoundland, and the Province of Canada (Upper and Lower Canada)—operated as separate units. By the 1860s, however, Upper Canadians began to push for a change. The British North America Act, passed by the British Parliament in 1867, divided the Province of Canada into two provinces, Ontario and Quebec, and joined them to New Brunswick and Nova Scotia under a strong federal government. The act also described the role of the central government and the duties of the individual provinces. On July 1, 1867, the Dominion of Canada became a confederation under England's Queen Victoria.

Under the new confederation each province had its own elected assembly. On the national level the Parliament—divided into the elected House of Commons and the appointed Senate—was set up according to the British system of government. The prime minister and the cabinet, chosen from the national Parliament, headed the federal government along with the governor-general, who represented the queen.

Eventually, all ten of Canada's provinces and its two territories (areas too sparsely populated to be organized as provinces) joined under the federal banner. In a friendly parting, Canada became an independent nation under the Statute of Westminster, passed by the British Parliament in 1931. Canada retained membership in the British Commonwealth. It was not until 1982, when Canada passed the Canada Act, that the nation gained the right to amend its own constitution.

Source: *Britannica Atlas*

LATIN AMERICA'S WARS OF INDEPENDENCE

Simón Bolívar, the orphaned son of a rich

Venezuelan family, learned early about self-government. His tutor, Simón Rodriguez, taught him the lessons of French philosopher Jean Jacques Rousseau —champion of representative government—when he was a young child. Rodriguez also taught by example: In 1797 the tutor had to flee Venezuela after being linked to a plot to set up a republican form of government.

The man who would one day free much of Latin America from Spain learned more lessons in Europe. In 1799, the young Latin American aristocrat visited Spain, where he saw the corruption of the royal family and felt the snubs of Spanish nobles. In France he saw the reforms that Napoleon Bonaparte had enacted there. During a second trip to Europe, Bolívar watched as the French emperor received the Italian crown. Inspired, Bolívar climbed to the top of Mount Sacro overlooking Rome and, kneeling, pledged to free Venezuela. It was a pledge he would keep.[1]

Toussaint L'Ouverture came out of hiding when Napoleon promised to negotiate. The French leader had him arrested and jailed.

In 1804 Haiti became the first Latin American nation to declare its independence. Napoleon had taken over the island nation from Spain in 1795. Haitian slaves, under the leadership of Toussaint L'Ouverture, rebelled in 1802 against French troops after the French general reneged on his promise to end slavery. Napoleon offered to make terms with Toussaint, then jailed the former slave when he came out of hiding. During a fierce race war that destroyed much of the nation's rich sugar crop, Jean-Jacques Dessalines, an ex-slave who had fought with Toussaint, took control of Haiti. He declared its independence on January 1, 1804.

Though the race war in Haiti horrified the creoles in Latin America, the spirit of revolution—in North America, France, and now at their doorstep—intrigued many. Two more world events would push them further into the republican camp.

In 1805 the British practically wiped out the Spanish navy during the Battle of Trafalgar. Napoleon had coerced Spain and Portugal into siding with France in its fight against the British. Without a strong navy, Spain could not send supplies and soldiers to its colonies in Latin America. Spain was no longer a world power.

In 1808 Napoleon invaded Spain and detained the royal family. Napoleon's brother, Joseph, assumed the throne as king of Spain. The Spanish people refused to accept Joseph as their king. Those who didn't have guns used axes, stones, and boiling water against the French soldiers.[2] Spanish leaders—many of them military chiefs—formed local committees, or *juntas*, to direct the revolt until Fernando, the son of the Spanish king, could reclaim the throne. Though Napoleon held control of Madrid, the juntas set up a *cortes*, or parliament, at a temporary capital in Cádiz. The Spanish colonies elected thirty representatives to serve on the cortes; Spain elected seventy-five.[3]

The cortes operated from 1810 to 1814. For a time, the Spanish colonies in Latin America continued to

Simón Bolívar: "Those who have served the cause of the revolution have plowed the sea."

run as usual under the viceroyalty system. Most people sympathized with Spain and remained loyal to Fernando. However, they soon objected to the number of delegates they were allowed to send to the cortes. The wealthy creoles wanted equal representation on the committee. Why, they asked, should they take orders from the Spanish cortes? Why not set up their own government until Fernando resumed power?

On July 5, 1811, a congress of wealthy Venezuelan creoles, led by Francisco de Miranda, declared their independence. The Republic of Venezuela survived only a year. Spanish officials ordered the harbors blocked, causing the new nation's economy to collapse. While many of the rich creoles living in the cities supported the independence movement, those in rural areas still pledged their loyalty to the king. A major earthquake in March 1812 delivered the final blow to the new republic. The quake leveled cities and killed thousands but ironically left standing many of the homes where those loyal to the king lived.[4] Spanish troops arrived from Cuba, defeated the remaining rebels, and sent Miranda to a Spanish jail where he died.

Similar moves toward independence began to appear in other areas of Latin America. Cabildas (town councilors) in Buenos Aires, Argentina, met on May 22, 1810, to set up a new government in La Plata. Three days later, a junta claimed the right to govern the province in King Fernando's name. In New Granada, the cabildas arrested the viceroy there and took over the government. The creole leaders were so disorganized, however, that the government of that period became known as *patria boba*, foolish fatherland.[5]

When Fernando regained the throne in Spain in 1814, many of the king's Latin American subjects cheered as loudly as his European followers. For a time the cause of independence lost ground.

But the movement's leaders had not given up. Simón Bolívar had set up a second republic in Venezuela after the collapse of the first, only to see it overrun by Spanish soldiers. Now he retreated to New Granada to rally his supporters. An inspiring leader, Bolívar convinced the freedom-loving cowboys who roamed the low plains of central Venezuela to join his soldiers. Great Britain, eager to open Latin American ports to English trade, supplied several thousand volunteer soldiers, guns, and other needed equipment.[6]

In 1817 Bolívar began his push from the north, while General José Francisco de San Martín led allied forces in the south. After months of exhausting marches across the rugged Andes and the harsh terrain of the plateau, the two rebel forces routed the Spanish. In 1818 San Martín and General Bernardo O'Higgins declared Chile's independence. Paraguay and Argentina soon followed. On June 24, 1821, Bolívar's forces defeated the Spaniards at Carabobo and in triumph proclaimed Venezuela's freedom. That same year, Antonio José Sucre and his soldiers beat back the royal forces in Ecuador and took over the government. One year later, most of New Granada was in the hands of the rebels.

Source: *Latin America: A General History*

San Martín established himself as Protector in Peru after the viceroy withdrew. But Spanish forces still threatened near Lima. In December 1824 Sucre led his army of 5,700 men high into the Andes. Facing them along the mountain ridges were 9,300 Spanish soldiers. The two generals greeted each other politely. The battle that followed lasted only a short time. Atop the imposing mountains, men dropped from altitude sickness as well as from wounds. When the battle cries ended, the Spanish had lost 1,600 men to the Latin Americans' 300.[7] Sucre's victory marked the end of the vast Peruvian empire Spain had ruled for three hundred years.

New Spain

In 1820 army officers in Spain rebelled against the inept rule of King Fernando. They forced him to adopt the Constitution of 1812, which had been created during Joseph Bonaparte's rule and which limited the king's power. Inspired by the Madrid revolt, the creoles in Mexico decided to try their own push for freedom. A bit of treachery helped them in their cause. Augustín de Iturbide, a Spanish army officer, offered to fight the rebels, but instead, he joined forces with them. In May 1822 Iturbide and his followers set up Mexico as a free country under a constitutional monarchy. Iturbide took the throne as emperor.

After ten months revolutionary forces led by Antonio López de Santa Anna drove Iturbide into exile. He was later executed. In November 1823 a new group of leaders, after lengthy debate, adopted a Mexican constitution. The document set up Mexico as a republic with a president (elected by the states), a congress, and a judicial system. The new United States of Mexico made Roman Catholicism the official religion and assured its citizens the rights of a free people. Guadalupe Victoria served as the country's first president. During the second election, Vincente Guerrero, who had fought with Iturbide for independence, seized power after winning only nine of the nineteen states. A series of strong leaders, including Santa Anna, would battle to control Mexico for the next thirty years.

A similar effort was under way in the rest of New Spain. The members of the provincial assembly declared the area independent on September 15, 1821. Spain, distracted by its internal struggles and the revolts in South America, did not oppose the move. Gabino Gaínza, the Spaniard who had served as captain-general of the region, took over as head of the government. The region joined with Mexico, but the union was not a happy one and soon dissolved.

Honduras, Guatemala, El Salvador, Nicaragua, and Costa Rica formed a republic under one central government after breaking with Mexico. The Federation of Central America, formed in 1823, soon came up against the same forces that would plague Latin American nations for years: a population not educated in self-government, ambitious military leaders, and angry underclasses. By 1839 the federation had broken up into five small, poor nations.

Mexican general Santa Anna signed a treaty with the United States conceding the lands of Texas in exchange for his life in 1836. He later unsuccessfully battled the Americans for control of the land during the Mexican War.

British Honduras, settled by English loggers in 1638, remained under that nation's protection. It was a British colony from 1862 until 1981, when it became the independent nation of Belize.

Cuba

By the 1830s Cuba was the last important colony still held by Spain. The Spanish government took strong measures to keep the island nation under control. It imposed harsh taxes on Cuban businesses and enforced strict laws on the people. The creole landowners' calls for reforms went unanswered. They were allowed no voice in the colonial government.

This high-handed treatment by Spain soon created resentment among the creoles. A ten-year revolt led by Carlos Manuel de Céspedes ended in failure. When Spain reneged on promised reforms, the poet patriot José Martí united the Cubans against the Spanish. Inspired by Martí, who was killed early in the war, the Cuban rebels fought against the Spanish army from 1895 to 1898.

The United States watched the revolt closely. Wary of a European nation's army ninety miles from their coast, many Americans favored the beleaguered Cubans. When the U.S.S. *Maine* exploded in the port of Havana, the United States blamed the act on the Spaniards and declared war on Spain. The Americans defeated the Spanish force in short order. After only a few months, the Spanish-American War ended, leaving Cuba in the hands of the Americans.

The U.S. Army remained on the island until 1902. At that time Cuba technically became an independent nation. But the country's powerful American protectors attached strings to Cuba's freedom. The U.S. Congress passed the Platt Amendment, which required Cuba to get American permission before making treaties or borrowing money from other countries. It also set up a U.S. military base on Cuba's Guantánamo Bay and allowed the United States to return to Cuba whenever necessary to keep the peace or to preserve its democratic government. Cuba included the provisions of the Platt Amendment in its constitution. Though the amendment was repealed in 1933, Cuba would not escape the influence of its powerful American neighbor.

Brazil

For three centuries, the monarchs of Portugal ruled Brazil in much the same manner as Spain had ruled Spanish America. When Napoleon took over Portugal in 1807, the royal family fled to Brazil. In 1815 Prince João declared Brazil equal to Portugal in status. The following year, when the queen died, João became king and ruled from his Brazilian home. When he returned to claim the throne after Napoleon's defeat, he left his son, Prince Pedro de Braganza, in charge of Brazil. By this time Portugal had adopted the Spanish constitution, giving more power to the parliament. These new Portuguese leaders feared Brazil's growing strength. In 1822 they demoted Brazil to its former colonial status and closed its ports to all nations except Portugal. They also demanded that Pedro return to Portugal.

The young ruler refused. On September 7, 1822, Brazil, led by its royal son, proclaimed its freedom from Portugal. On December 1, 1822, the twenty-four-year-old Pedro was crowned emperor of Brazil. Portugal took no action against the new monarchy.

In 1824 Pedro I appointed a committee that prepared a constitution for the new nation. After local councils approved the pact, it became the law of the land in March 1824. The new constitution gave the emperor the power to run the government. A parliament with two houses made laws. The members of the upper house, called the senate, were selected by the emperor from a list provided by the provinces and served for life. The members of the lower house, the chamber of deputies, were elected by voters in the district. Only adult males who owned property could vote. Each province had its own president, appointed by the emperor, and an elected council who advised the president. Under the constitution, the emperor had the power to override the parliament and the court. This system of government ruled Brazil for sixty-five years.

Pedro I served as emperor of Brazil for seven years. He had his critics, and in 1831 he returned to Portugal. Pedro II, the emperor's five-year-old son, inherited the throne. A three-man regency ruled on behalf of the young king until 1835. Father Diogo Antonio Feijó took over the job for the next two years. He was followed by Pedro de Araújo Lima, who ruled until Pedro assumed the throne at age fifteen. Crowned in 1841, Pedro II served for forty-eight years. Under his rule, Brazil's economy grew dramatically. The Latin American-born ruler allowed freedom of religion and freed Brazil's slaves. The latter action cost him his crown. Landowners, angry over the loss of their slaves, banded together with the army and forced the emperor to abdicate in 1889.

Pedro II left behind a nation with a strong economy and a growing population. Brazil, alone among the Latin American viceroyalties, remained united as one nation.

Pedro II was fifteen years old when he took over rule of Brazil as emperor.

CHAPTER FIVE

SELF-GOVERNMENT

Having separated themselves from Europe, the independent nations of the Western Hemisphere took their place in the world. Once liberated, however, the nations traveled widely different roads. Though plagued by occasional uprisings and, in the case of the United States, a civil war, the two northern countries of the North American continent followed a steady course. Their form of government has changed little over the years. They have avoided an overthrow of the government; the people of both the United States and Canada continue to have a say in their government.

Almost all the Latin American countries, however, have endured years of upheaval. With few exceptions, these nations have suffered under repressive regimes. Military coups, revolts led by military men, have repeatedly overthrown elected governments. Military coups took over the Bolivian government 189 times

At left, thousands gather in front of the U.S. Capitol in January 1993 to view the first inauguration of Bill Clinton as the forty-second president of the United States.

between its independence in 1825 to 1980.[1] Dictators have thrown out constitutions and passed their own laws. Many Latin American nations continue to struggle with uprisings and pressures from the military.

Why were the northern nations able to sustain stable governments while the nations to the south were plagued by almost constant unrest? One reason is that the North Americans—as former subjects of England—had years of training in self-government before declaring independence. A free press, well-established in the British colonies by the end of the 1700s, served as a vital part of that training. Newspapers and flyers—supporting, attacking, and informing—circulated freely. Their readers became accustomed to questioning government actions and to judging public officials for themselves.

Another part of the answer lies in the constitutions adopted by the nations of the Western Hemisphere and the way in which the people of each country view them. When a constitution remains in place, it provides stability and security. People know what is expected of them and their leaders. All know they must live by the rule of law. Regimes that cast aside their nation's constitution at will undermine their peoples' faith in government. Without permanent laws, people have no assurance that their rights will be protected.

U.S. GOVERNMENT

The U.S. Constitution is the oldest federal constitution in the world. Most of the nations in the Western Hemisphere and many elsewhere have used it as a model for their own constitutions. It has survived more than two centuries of rapid change, a civil war that bitterly divided the nation's people, two world wars, and protests over civil rights and America's role in the Vietnam War. It held the nation together as two presidents faced impeachment and eight more were killed or died in office. Having the nation's rulebook firmly in place assured that the mantle of power passed peacefully to the next in line.

For the first years of its existence as an independent nation, the United States operated as a confederation of thirteen strong, independent states. By 1785 it was clear to at least some of the founders that a strong government was needed to hold the new nation together. The Articles of Confederation, which the founders had drawn up during the Revolutionary War, had formed a union of the thirteen states and given the federal government powers that enabled it to run the war. But under the articles, the federal government had no power to enforce laws, levy taxes, or make treaties unless all the individual states agreed. Each state could issue its own paper money, establish relations with Indian tribes in its territory, and engage in trade wars with its neighbors.

After the war, the limitations on the federal government began to threaten the existence of the union. Without tax money from the states, the nation could not pay off debts or maintain its navy. Treaties were practically worthless because individual states could ignore their terms. Instead of negotiating with the federal government, foreign countries, like England and Spain, began dealing directly with the states.[2]

Despite the problems, states were suspicious of a strong federal government and reluctant to give up any of their power. After much persuasion by James Madison, Alexander Hamilton, and others, the state legislators agreed to hold a Constitutional Convention in May 1787 to strengthen the federal government.

After months of compromise, the delegates at last adopted a Constitution. In just seven articles, the document spelled out the workings of a new government, established a strong central government, and protected the rights of the states and their people. On September 17, 1787, thirty-nine delegates signed the Constitution. Three did not: two Virginians and the crusty critic from Massachusetts, Elbridge Gerry.[3]

Though the states ratified the Constitution, many citizens still felt uneasy about giving power to a strong central government. To protect against an abuse of power, they believed the Constitution should spell out their rights.

James Madison agreed and drew up amendments to the Constitution to guarantee citizens' rights. These first ten amendments, called the Bill of Rights, went into effect on December 15, 1791. They give citizens the right to free speech, to circulate petitions against government actions, to participate in peaceful protests, to bear arms, to worship as they please, to be free from unreasonable search and seizure, and to have a trial by jury. They provide for a free press and allow states to establish their own militias. The tenth amendment reserves for the states or the people all rights not specifically granted to the federal government.

These rights cannot be overridden by either the president or Congress. The Supreme Court is the guardian of these rights. When reviewing laws and cases before the court, the justices must consider whether they violate the Constitution or the Bill of Rights.

When the founders wrote the U.S. Constitution, they knew that the country and the world would undergo radical changes in the future. They designed the constitution so that future generations could amend it to fit the times. But they made the process difficult, so that the constitution couldn't be altered at whim or by one faction. Since the adoption of the Bill of Rights, the Constitution has been amended only sixteen times. The most recent amendment gave eighteen-year-olds the right to vote. To amend the Constitution, two-thirds of both houses of Congress must approve a proposed change. Before it can take effect, an amendment must be approved by three-fourths of the state legislatures.

This is in stark contrast to what happens in many other countries. Brazil adopted its eighth constitution in 1988 and began efforts to revise it just a few years later.[4] An earlier constitution that took power away from congress and gave more power to the president was enacted in 1967 by Brazilian military rulers. That consti-

"I consider the popular election of one branch of the national legislature as essential to free government." — *James Madison*

tution also banned opposing political parties. The country's rulers tortured critics of the new constitution and harassed church leaders who opposed it.[5]

In several other Latin American countries, dictators and military coups have suspended their nations' constitutions or discarded them altogether.

To ensure that no one segment of the government gained control, the framers of the U.S. Constitution set up three separate and equal branches of government: the executive, the legislative, and the judicial. The balance of power held by these three branches is one of the key ingredients of the U.S. democratic system. The executive branch is headed by the president and includes the vice president and the members of the Cabinet; the legislative branch consists of the House of Representatives and the Senate (together known as Congress); and the judicial branch refers to the federal court system and the Supreme Court.

Each branch has power over the others. A president can veto, or reject, bills passed by Congress. Congress and the president can move to impeach judges from their posts or make cuts in the federal court system. Congress, by a two-thirds vote, can override a presidential veto and can impeach and try a president for "treason, bribery, or other high crimes and misdemeanors." The Senate can reject the president's nominees, and Congress can refuse to finance executive programs. The Supreme Court can declare the acts of Congress or the president unconstitutional.

Members of either the House or the Senate may introduce a bill; however, only the House can introduce legislation to raise money and only the Senate can ratify treaties and vote on presidential appointments. For a bill to become a law, it must win a majority of votes from the House and the Senate and be signed by the president. A two-thirds majority of Congress can pass a bill that is rejected, or vetoed, by the president.

The 435 members of the House of Representatives are elected every two years. Each state is allotted representatives based on the number of people living within its borders. Senators, two for each state (one hundred in all), are elected for six-year terms. Under the Seventeenth Amendment to the Constitution, passed in 1913, citizens vote directly for senators. Before that, each state's legislators chose senators.

All citizens eighteen or older are entitled to vote except those who have been convicted of serious crimes. Voters are not required to own property or pass certain tests, although in the early days of the republic, only white men with property could vote.

Every four years, Americans elect a president. Several months before the election, which is held in November, the Democrats and the Republicans hold national conventions to select their candidates. Smaller political parties sometimes select candidates for the office of president as in 1996 when the Reform Party held a convention for the first time and selected Ross Perot as its candidate. Candidates not connected with a major party can appear on the ballot by collecting a certain number of signatures in each state.

THE SOLDIER CLAIMS CONTROL

On March 30, 1981, John Hinckley Jr. shot U.S. President Ronald Reagan and three other men outside a Washington hotel. The bullet punctured the president's lung.

The shooting, which occurred at 2:30 p.m., set in motion a series of events that demonstrated the strength of the American constitutional system of government.

Immediately after he heard of the shooting, Secretary of State Alexander Haig Jr. rushed to the White House. As a former commander of the North Atlantic Treaty Organization's forces, Haig was well used to giving orders in times of emergency. He headed for the Situation Room, the command central in the basement of the White House, where top officials were gathering. Vice President George Bush was on his way to Washington from Houston, where he had been on a speaking tour.

As Secretary of Defense Caspar Weinberger and other members of the Cabinet watched the reports of Reagan's ordeal on the White House television, Haig slipped out of the room. Suddenly, the TV cameras zeroed in on Haig as he stood clutching the podium in the White House Press Room a few doors away.

At 4:15 p.m., Haig, pale and perspiring, announced to the world that, "As of now, I am in control here in the White House, pending return of the Vice President, and in close touch with him. If something came up, I would check with him of course." Haig told reporters that he was assuming command because a new crisis management plan created by the Reagan team had placed him in line after the vice president, who had not yet arrived at the White House.

"Constitutionally, gentlemen," he said, "you have the President, the Vice President and the Secretary of State in that order."

Here was a former military man, announcing to the world, as the president of the United States lay wounded in a nearby hospital, that he was in control. In another nation, such an event might well have meant that the president had been deposed by a military coup. But in the United States, no one worried for a minute that Haig was actu-

Alexander Haig Jr.

ally trying to take over command. Despite Haig's misinformed statement, the Constitution guarantees that the vice president, then the Speaker of the House and the Senate President Pro Tem stand in line, in that order, to assume leadership should the president die or be incapacitated. The secretary of state is fifth in line of succession.

Presidential aides later said Haig was only trying to reassure the nation and other countries of the world that the U.S. government would continue to operate despite the crisis. Haig's brashness, however, earned him unending criticism and an angry rebuke from Secretary of Defense Caspar Weinberger, who quickly said he was in charge of the nation's military, not Haig. Vice President Bush arrived at the White House at 6:59 p.m. and took over the reins of government without opposition. Throughout the ordeal, Reagan remained president, with Bush acting as his assistant until he recovered.

The New York Times

Under the Constitution, citizens don't vote directly for presidential candidates in the election. Instead, each state's voters elect members of the electoral college. On some state's ballots, only the names of the presidential and vice presidential candidates are listed. The voters, however, are really voting for the electors who favor those candidates.

These electors choose the president and vice president after the November election has taken place. The number of electors allotted each state is equal to the number of representatives and senators that state has. In addition, the District of Columbia is entitled to three electoral votes. Electors don't have to vote for the candidate they supported on the ballot, but they almost always do. In all but three cases (1824, 1876, and 1888), the candidate who received the most votes in the November election has won the presidency.

Elected governors serve as chief executives of the states. Elected legislatures, each with two houses (except the one-house legislature in Nebraska), direct the affairs of the state. On the local level, elected county and municipal officials and councils take care of matters in their areas.

The U.S. Constitution set up an independent Supreme Court with power equal to that of the president and the Congress. As such, it is the most powerful court in the world. The Supreme Court has nine justices, appointed for life by the president and approved by two-thirds of the Senate. Each justice has one vote; a final decision must be approved by a majority of the justices hearing the case. The Court rules on cases appealed from lower courts, on disputes between states or between a state and the federal government, and on matters involving interpretation of the Constitution. Citizens may override Supreme Court decisions only by passing an amendment to the Constitution.

CANADIAN GOVERNMENT

Like their U.S. neighbors, Canadians have long lived by the rule of law. The Canadian government is largely based on the English Parliamentary system. The nation's constitution, detailed in the Canada Act of 1982 and the Charter of Rights and Freedoms, spells out the powers of the federal and provincial governments and the rights and duties of citizens. Canadians are guaranteed the right to life and liberty; freedom of religion, of speech, and of the press; and the right to assemble peacefully and to associate with whomever they wish.

Other rules of government—such as those relating to marriage and other civil matters—are contained in the unwritten traditions of the English system. At least seven of Canada's ten provinces and more than half of its voters must approve changes to the constitution.

Queen Elizabeth II, ruler of the British Commonwealth of Nations, serves as Canada's head of state. She is represented in Canada by the governor-general, who is recommended by the prime minister and appointed

The Canadian Charter of Rights and Freedoms says: Everyone has the following fundamental freedoms: (a) freedom of conscience and religion; (b) freedom of thought, belief, opinion and expression, including freedom of the press and other means of communication; (c) freedom of peaceful assembly; and (d) freedom of association.

by the queen. The governor-general usually serves from five to seven years. The post is now largely ceremonial. The true power lies with Parliament.

Divided into two houses, Parliament directs the workings of the federal government. The 295 members of the lower house, known as the House of Commons, are elected by the voters, citizens eighteen years or older. Each province is allotted a set number of house members based on population.

The 104-member Senate is appointed by the governor-general, following the recommendations of the prime minister. Members used to be appointed for life; they now must retire at age seventy-five. Senators come from all regions of Canada, with the most populous provinces generally having the most members. Each of Canada's two territories, the Northwest Territories and the Yukon Territory, has one member in the Senate.

The Parliament oversees national defense, foreign trade and foreign relations, money and banking, unemployment insurance, criminal law, broadcasting, agriculture, immigration, pensions, and other matters not assigned to the provinces.

Members of either chamber of Parliament may introduce a bill except that bills involving taxes and revenue must originate in the House of Commons. Each chamber must approve a bill before it becomes law. Although the Senate has the power to veto bills introduced in the House of Commons, it rarely does. Once a bill has been passed by both chambers, it is signed into law by the governor-general. Traditionally, the governor-general always signs bills approved by both chambers.

The prime minister is the political head of the government. He or she is a member of Parliament and the head of the political party with the majority of seats in the House of Commons. If no party has a majority of seats in Parliament, a prime minister's party may join forces with other parties to win enough support to continue in office. This is called a coalition.

To help run the government, a cabinet of approximately thirty members is selected by the prime minister from the House of Commons (and occasionally from the Senate). Each cabinet member heads a governmental department, such as finance or justice.

The prime minister and the cabinet—as leaders of the majority party—hold much of the power in the government. They dictate the bills they want passed. Members of the majority party in Parliament usually follow the position taken by the leadership. Those who do not may be drummed out of the party or may lose support for pet projects.

By law, the prime minister must call a new election at least every five years. Frequently, a prime minister will call an election earlier than required. An early election is usually called for one of two reasons:

1) The prime minister and his party have strong support from voters in the polls. By holding an early election, the prime minister ensures that his party will hold power for another term.

2) Opposition parties succeed in winning enough

support among Parliament members to defeat a major bill sponsored by the prime minister. The prime minister is not required to call an early election if that happens, but such a loss indicates the prime minister no longer commands the support of the majority party members in Parliament. Without support, the prime minister won't be able to accomplish anything. A new election may replace dissenting members with candidates more favorable to the prime minister's views. Or voters may reject the prime minister and the majority party in favor of opposition leaders.

The government of the provinces operates much like the national Parliament. The queen is represented by a lieutenant governor in each province, appointed by the governor-general. A premier heads the provincial government. He or she is chosen in the same way as the prime minister. Each province has its own elected legislature, known as the Legislative Assembly, which has only one house. Quebec refers to its chief executive as the prime minister; its legislature is the National Assembly. Provinces control taxes, law enforcement, education, and other regional matters.

In the Northwest Territories, a commissioner appointed by the federal government and an elected council oversee law enforcement, education, and medical care in their region. The Yukon Territory is similarly run by an elected government leader and an elected council.

Local government is administered by elected councils, headed by elected mayors, wardens, or overseers.

Canadian Prime Minister Pierre Trudeau, seated left, signs the Canada Act in Ottawa in 1982 as Queen Elizabeth II, seated right, looks on.

Canada's court system is set up much like the U.S. judiciary. Provincial courts hear cases involving crimes and civil matters occurring within the region. Federal courts hear claims concerning federal laws. Cases from both courts may be appealed to the Canadian Supreme Court. The governor-general, following the recommendations of the prime minister, appoints all judges. Nine justices, appointed to life terms, serve on the Supreme Court, the highest court in Canada.

LATIN AMERICAN GOVERNMENTS

Emerging from their bondage to European monarchs, Latin American nations searched for ways to govern their lands. Many adopted constitutions based on the U.S. Constitution. They set up democracies and held elections. Even with a written constitution, however, many of these nations failed in their attempts to establish stable governments. Years of violence, repression, and corruption followed. Some nations remain in the grip of unstable governments today.

Unlike their North American neighbors, the nations of Latin America lacked experience in self-government. The defeated tribes, the black slaves, and their descendants had never had a say in colonial government. Even the wealthy landowners had not been schooled in self-government. Only the peninsulares had participated in government, but many of them returned to Spain and Portugal after their terms of office were over or during the wars of independence.

In a rare attempt at self-rule, escaped black slaves established a settlement known as Palmares in the forests of northeast Brazil in the 1630s. The community, which survived for more than sixty years, had an elected king and a council. In 1694 soldiers hired by the colonial governor destroyed Palmares, killing the king and many others.

These nations had not operated under the rule of law. All power had centered on the monarch and the monarch's ministers in the New World. The laws governing the nations had been changed according to the whims of the leader in charge. Even *El Libertador*, the great freedom fighter Simón Bolívar, took over as dictator of the Republic of Colombia when others refused to support his push for a strong central government.

This tradition of strong rulers opened the door to dictators, who ignored written laws and grabbed power for themselves as the monarchs before them had done. Dictators, some backed by military coups, simply discarded constitutions and wrote their own.

The central role of the military made it easier for dictators to seize control. Today, the military continues to hold a position of power in many Latin American countries. One exception is Costa Rica, where the army was abolished in 1949 and replaced by a civil guard. That nation, a democratic republic, has had one of the most stable governments in Latin America.

Bad economic conditions, which continue to plague Latin America even now, made it harder for elected governments to retain control. People, desperate for food and shelter, went along with leaders who promised better times. When declining markets and skyrocketing foreign debts threatened the economy of Brazil in the 1930s, military leaders installed Getulio Vargas as president. During his fifteen years as dictator, Vargas suspended the nation's constitution and extended his term of office.

A member of the Brazilian military police threatens street children in 1990. In Brazil, as in many Latin American nations, the military enforces the law.

Similar conditions affected the United States, but leaders were held in check by the balance of powers written into the Constitution. When the Great Depression threatened the nation's economy, President Franklin D. Roosevelt used his influence to push radical social programs through Congress. Part of his program was ruled unconstitutional by the Supreme Court. Roosevelt tried to use his presidential powers to add justices who favored his views to the Court. Citizens and Congress opposed Roosevelt's plan to reorganize the Court, and the proposal was dropped.

Frustrated by lack of any real role in their governments, Latin Americans have often resorted to violence. For years, Colombians swung unsteadily between dictators and elected leaders. A cycle developed. A collapse in the economy or other crisis weakened the elected leader's rule. Taking advantage of the situation, terrorists threatened the nation with chaos. A dictator or a junta—a group of military officers— seized control. The new regime regained order but trampled citizens' rights. Citizens, backed by another military group, forced an election, and the cycle repeated itself.

After citizens revolted against Bolívar's regime, his deputy Francisco de Paula Santander set up a constitutional government in Colombia. In 1880 a dictator assumed control. At the beginning of the twentieth century, Colombians waged the War of a Thousand Days, a battle between liberal and conservative forces that claimed more than 100,000 lives.[6]

Half a century later, Colombian radicals sparked another violent episode after a popular leftist leader was killed. Known as "La Violencia," the terrorist siege lasted for a decade, destroyed the capital city, and killed 200,000 people.[7] Finally, in 1958 members of Colombia's Conservative and Liberal parties agreed to share power. For the next sixteen years, the presidency rotated between the two parties.

Technically, Colombia is considered a democratic republic. Power is divided among executive, legislative, and judicial branches. The president, elected directly by voters, serves a four-year term and cannot immediately run for reelection. A thirteen-member cabinet and an advisory board called the Council of State appointed by the president assist in running the government. The president has the power to approve or veto laws passed by the Congress.

The National Congress, divided into a Chamber of Representatives and a Senate, operates much like the U.S. Congress. Voters, who must be eighteen or older, elect its members to four-year terms. Each department, or state, is represented by two senators and two chamber members plus additional representatives based on population.

Colombia's twenty-three departments are headed by governors appointed by the president. Voters elect mayors and councils to run local governments.

Colombia also has an independent court system. However, drug lords, who control a large part of the nation's economy, have used bribes and assassinations to influence and intimidate judges and other officials.[8] Violence and lawlessness continue to undermine the effectiveness of the government.

In 1974 voters elected a liberal president in the country's first open election in more than twenty years. But by the 1980s, terrorists, financed by drug lords, had taken control of the society. In 1985 a group of terrorists stormed the Palace of Justice wielding grenades and automatic weapons. The army took back the court building, but eleven Supreme Court justices and numerous court workers died in the attack.

Colombia's story is not unusual. The list of dictators, military coups, takeovers, and assassinations in the rest of Latin America is lengthy.

During the 1950s, military coups took over the governments of Argentina, Venezuela, Colombia, Brazil, and Peru. Fidel Castro toppled Cuba's dictator in the late 1950s and sent revolutionary squads throughout Latin America. Battles between communists and anti-communists raged in Nicaragua, Honduras, El Salvador, and Guatemala into the 1990s. In 1973, a military coup killed Chile's socialist president, Salvador Allende Gossens, elected by voters in 1970. Mexico, where one party ruled from 1929 to 1997, is rife with charges of election fraud, corruption, and drug lords.

Today, many Latin American countries are democratic republics [see chart on page 12]. Nevertheless, many continue to be plagued by political intrigue. Corruption, economic downturns, voter fraud, and repression threaten their stability.

In Colombia, citizens who are at least eighteen years old are required to vote. Similar laws are in effect in several other Latin American nations.

CHAPTER SIX

ALL IN THE NEIGHBORHOOD

For almost two centuries, the United States has been an active participant in Central and South American affairs. In 1808 President Thomas Jefferson told Mexican leaders the United States supported their struggle for independence. When Latin American nations finally separated themselves from Spain and Portugal, the United States was among the first to recognize their independence.

On December 2, 1823, President James Monroe issued a warning to the European nations not to try to regain their former colonies in the Western Hemisphere. Since then, American leaders have cited the Monroe Doctrine many times when ordering U.S. troops to Latin American nations. In 1833 U.S. forces went to Argentina to put down a rebellion. Three years later, they were sent to Peru. During the second half of the 1800s, U.S. forces landed on Latin American soil almost fifty times.[1]

At left, a U.S. marine guards the front of the Panamanian Defense Forces station in La Chorrera during the U.S. invasion of Panama in 1989.

In 1864 France declared Mexico an empire and placed Maximilian, archduke of Austria, on the throne as emperor. The United States, in the midst of the Civil War, did not respond at first to this violation of the Monroe Doctrine. At the war's end, France left Mexico after U.S. troops marched to the Rio Grande. Mexicans later executed Maximilian.

Under President Theodore Roosevelt, the United States saw itself as the Western Hemisphere's official law enforcer. In 1905 the United States assumed control of a debt-ridden Dominican Republic when European nations threatened to occupy the island nation until their loans were repaid. For the next seventeen years, the U.S. Marines and then the Navy oversaw that nation's administration.

During the Spanish-American War, the United States helped Cuba and Puerto Rico in their fight against the Spanish. At the war's end, however, U.S. forces remained in both nations. The American army left Cuba in 1902, but returned for two years in 1906 when political turmoil threatened the nation. Until 1933, a U.S. law (the Platt Amendment) allowed American troops to return to Cuba to prevent turmoil.

In 1958 Fidel Castro and his band of rebels overthrew the dictatorship of Fulgencio Batista. When Castro allied with the Soviet Union, the U.S. Central Intelligence Agency sponsored an invasion of Cuba at the Bahia de los Cochinos (Bay of Pigs) in 1961. The plan was a disaster and boosted Castro's image in the world. During the Cuban Missile Crisis the following year, the Soviets agreed to withdraw their missiles from the island. But the United States had to pledge in return not to invade Cuba.

A U.S. territory since the Spanish-American War, Puerto Rico became a commonwealth in 1952. Puerto Rican residents are U.S. citizens who have their own constitution and elect a governor and a legislature.

Puerto Ricans cannot vote for U.S. presidents, and their representative in Congress has no vote. Puerto Ricans pay no U.S. income tax, but they do pay income taxes to Puerto Rico.

For years, the population has been divided on whether the island should become a state (which requires approval by two-thirds of the population and a vote by the U.S. Congress) or remain a commonwealth. A small minority (less than 5 percent) support independence. So passionate are people about the issue that cafés in Puerto Rico post signs that say "No talking about politics allowed."[2]

The United States' relationship with Panama dates back to 1903 when Americans wanted to build a canal there. At that time, Panama was part of Colombia. When Colombia refused to allow the United States to take over the land needed for the canal, Americans encouraged Panama to break away from Colombia. In more recent times, U.S. troops invaded Panama in 1989 and helped Panamanians crush the military government. General Manuel Noriega, who controlled the government at that time, was later convicted in the United States for his role in drug trafficking.

American leaders have supported dictators, guerrillas, nationalist movements, and others in Nicaragua, Honduras, Haiti, Guatemala, and El Salvador in their efforts to prevent communists from gaining a foothold in the Western Hemisphere. Like many other world powers, the United States uses foreign aid to influence Latin American politics. Latin American governments

ATTACK ON THE HOUSE FLOOR

On March 1, 1954, at 2:32 p.m., 243 members of the U.S. House of Representatives had just begun to vote on a bill that would allow Mexican farm workers into the country during harvest time.

Without warning, three Puerto Rican nationalists, leaning from a spectators' gallery above the House floor, began spraying the room with automatic weapon fire. As members of Congress stood frozen in horror, Lolita Lebron, holding a loaded German Luger in both hands, aimed into the air and fired. When the bullets were spent, she tossed the gun to a companion, waved the Puerto Rican flag, and shouted, "Viva Puerto Rico! Freedom for my country." Her accomplices, Rafael C. Miranda, Irving Flores-Rodriguez, and Andres Cordero, continued firing.

Below, a congressman shouted, "Hit the deck!" Some obeyed, throwing themselves on the floor or hiding behind chairs. Others, stunned, stood still as bullets crashed into chairs and tables around them. One bullet missed the House leader by less than a foot; another buried itself in a chair next to the minority leader.

In the gallery, tourists who had come for a firsthand look at government in action, cowered behind the shooters. Two spectators, a House clerk, and a seventy-one-year-old doorman jumped the gunmen and Lebron as they tried to escape, their guns still smoking. Representative James Van Zandt ran up the steps to the gallery and helped muscle one of the terrorists to the floor. Lebron's shrill voice cut through the shouts and commotion, repeating her demands for "freedom."

As bullets whizzed through the air, four Congressmen fell to the House floor. A fifth, Ben Jensen, a Republican from Iowa, staggered into a cloakroom before collapsing. Two congressmen who were doctors examined their injuries. Representative Alvin Bentley, bleeding heavily from wounds in the lung, liver, and stomach, was the most seriously hurt in the attack. He later recovered.

The shooters, all New York residents, were members of the Puerto Rico Nationalists, a fanatical party that supported independence for Puerto Rico. The party was founded in 1928 by Pedro Albizu Campos, a Harvard graduate and political activist in Puerto Rico. Members of the group had been involved in an assassination attempt on President Harry Truman in 1950 and after the House attack were implicated in a plot to kill President Dwight Eisenhower. Ironically, both presidents had supported independence for Puerto Rico if the voters there approved the move.

Police arresting Lebron found a note in her purse that read: "The United States of America are betraying the sacred principles of mankind in their continuous subjugation of my country, violating their rights to be a free nation and a free people."

The shooting got attention but little support for the nationalist cause. Puerto Rican leaders, repudiating the attack, claimed that no more than 150 people belonged to the group. The terrorists were convicted and jailed for their actions.

As a result of the shooting, however, the United States tightened security in its public buildings. Visitors now must pass through metal detectors before entering most government buildings in Washington. But on that day in 1954, the nationalists had only to ask the guard if they could enter the gallery. Before he allowed them in, the guard asked them if they had cameras. They said they didn't.   *The New York Times* in favor receive money and trade advantages; those in opposition lose such aid. The United States banned trade with Haiti and Cuba to try to force changes in their governments. Nations affected by such embargoes often suffer great losses in their economies.

In the late 1970s, the United States became embroiled in a civil war between government forces in El Salvador. U.S. aid funded the government because of its anti-Communist stance, even though it was linked to death squads that terrorized and killed civilians. By the time the war ended in 1992, it had cost the lives of 80,000 El Salvadorans and resulted in an estimated $1 billion in damages. In a similar battle in Nicaragua, the United States backed anti-Communist rebels (contras) against government forces (Sandinistas).

The United States offers many reasons for its participation in Latin American affairs. The Monroe Doctrine was an attempt to assert the independence of the nations of the Western Hemisphere from Europe's monarchs. In it, the United States offered its protection to the new Latin American nations struggling to be free. American troops have helped quell rebellions and prevent massive destruction in countries such as Haiti and the Dominican Republic. Other measures have been taken to protest human rights abuses or to stop the spread of communism.

Critics of American policy blame the United States for the political turmoil in Latin America. Americans, they say, should let Latin Americans settle their own affairs.

A Nicaraguan contra rebel, equipped with ammunition belts and a rusty machine gun, patrols the hill country of northern Nicaragua.

The future of Latin America is uncertain. The nations there still struggle with poverty, hunger, and disease. Many of their people cannot read or write. Their economies, dependent on one or two products, rise and fall unpredictably.

There are signs of hope, however, that Latin Americans are at last taking control of their governments. The people and their leaders are learning to settle disputes in the halls of government rather than on the streets, with ballots instead of guns. As a result, the rule of law—not of dictators—is taking hold. Ecuador, El Salvador, Peru, Uruguay, Brazil, Chile, and several other Latin American nations now have stable governments that represent the citizens and guard their rights. Costa Rica has had only one dictator since its independence in 1821 and has had free elections since 1889.[3]

With this new stability comes true independence. As they learn to solve their own problems, Latin American nations are also better able to stand firm against interference from other powers. Ecuador's resolution of a crisis in its government is a good example of that.

A small country in the northwestern corner of South America, Ecuador has been a democracy under civilian rule since 1979. A constitution approved by voters in 1978 set up a government with executive, legislative, and judicial branches. However, the National Congress has the power to fire members of the cabinet, who with the president and vice president, comprise the executive department.

During the last two decades, Ecuador has endured worker unrest, a president who surrounded the Supreme Court with tanks to prevent members from being sworn into office, and attacks from terrorist groups. A stagnant economy plagued the country in the late 1980s.

In February 1997 Ecuadoran workers throughout the nation staged a forty-eight-hour strike to protest the erratic behavior of the president, Abdala Bucaram, and to demand his ouster. In response, Congress voted to remove the president, who referred to himself as "El loco" (the crazy one), on the grounds of "mental incapacity." Vice president Rosalia Arteaga filled the office for three days until Congress voted to replace her with Fabian Alarcon. The actions caused a national furor, with Bucaram, Arteaga, and Alarcon all claiming to be head of state.

Military leaders stepped in and negotiated a settlement that called for the temporary appointment of Alarcon as president, with new elections scheduled in February 1998. Congress voted by more than a two-thirds majority to approve the plan.

Critics of Congress's actions—including the vice president—charged that the ouster and the replacement of the president were unconstitutional. However, the nation's constitution is unclear on whether Congress has the right to take such steps and on how a presidential vacancy is to be filled. Despite the criticism, observers were encouraged by three aspects of the episode:

- A new leader was installed by vote of Congress, not by a military coup. Although the military played an active role in the affair, military leaders refused to take over the government and said they never considered a coup.[4] During the crisis, no dictator moved in to take control.

- Congress set new elections and made it clear the interim president would be required to step down after voters elect a new president.

- No other nation was involved in the ouster and naming of a new president.

To Andres Perez, a leading Ecuadoran businessman who supported Congress's actions, the process meant progress. "It may be stretching the constitution," he noted, "but the people went to Congress to ask for the removal of a president. They did not go to the armed forces; they did not go to the embassy of the United States. They went to Congress."[5]

Observers look at Ecuador's experience as a hopeful sign that the nations of Latin America may at last be turning away from government by violence and toward the rule of law. As they head into the twenty-first century, it is hoped that Latin America, like their neighbors to the north, can at last adopt stable governments, guarantee the rights of their citizens, and make peaceful transitions from one leader to the next.

GLOSSARY

audiencia	high court in Spain's New World colonies
cabilda	town council in Spanish America; responsible for town government but really had little power
calpullis	clans, or family groups, in Aztec tribes
coalition	united front formed when two or more units join forces; used in Canada by two or more minority political parties to gain enough power to rule
commonwealth	alliance of independent nations, linked by common heritage; one leader serves as head of alliance
communism	system in which property and goods are shared and owned by all, based on the writings of Karl Marx; often enforced by totalitarian rule
confederation	alliance of independent groups that join together to address matters that concern them all; each group retains its own laws and leader
conquistador	Spanish (or Portuguese) conqueror in the New World
constitution	written document that sets down the rules of government and establishes the rights of citizens
corregidor	official who ruled towns in Spanish America and oversaw villages where native tribes lived
cortes	committee or parliament formed in 1810 to govern Spain when France forced the king to abdicate
coup	seizure of power, usually by members of the military
creole	Spaniard born in the New World
democracy	system of government by the people in which citizens elect representatives to govern; **presidential democracy** has an elected president as its head of state; **parliamentary democracy** is ruled by an elected parliament

dictator	leader who rules with absolute power
egalitarian society	system in which every member has an equal say
electoral college	group of electors selected by the states that chooses the president and vice president of the United States
executive branch	head of state (**president** or **prime minister**), federal governmental departments, and **cabinet** of advisers
impeachment	process by which the U.S. House of Representatives charges officials with misconduct; the Senate conducts the trial resulting from the charges
judicial branch	court system
junta	local committees set up in Spain to lead the revolt against France in the early 1800s; later used to refer to a group of military leaders holding power after a coup
legislative branch	representative body, such as **Congress** or **Parliament**
mestizo	Latin American of Spanish and Indian ancestry
monarchy	system of government ruled absolutely by a king or queen; a **limited** or **constitutional monarchy** exists when power is limited by constitution or code of law
nomads	people who wander through an area in search of food
peninsulares	Spanish-born officials in Latin America
province	individual region; in Canada, similar to a U.S. state
republic	form of democratic government based on a constitution; leaders in a republic are elected by the people and there is no hereditary ruler
totalitarian state	region or nation ruled absolutely by one person or group of persons; individuals are inferior to the state
veto	reject a bill
viceroy	represented European monarch, oversaw viceroyalty
viceroyalty	Spanish and Portuguese districts in the New World

SOURCE NOTES

INTRODUCTION: GOVERNING A NATION

1. "Washington's Farewell Address," *Compton's Encyclopedia*, vol. 25 (F.E. Compton Co., 1985), 26.

CHAPTER TWO: NATIVE RULE

1. John Edwin Fagg, *Latin America: A General History*, 2nd ed. (New York: Macmillan, 1969), 14.

2. Ibid, 15.

3. Ibid, 17.

4. Ibid., 25.

5. *The 1995 Grolier Multimedia Encyclopedia* (Grolier Electronic Publishing, Inc., 1995).

6. Ibid.

7. Catherine Owens Peare, *William Penn: A Biography* (New York: J. B. Lippincott Co., 1956), 254.

CHAPTER THREE: COLONIAL PERIOD

1. " 'The Mayflower'—Its Famous Voyage," *Compton's Encyclopedia*, vol. 14 (F.E. Compton Co., 1985), 183.

2. Ann E. Weiss, *Good Neighbors? The U.S. and Latin America* (Boston: Houghton Mifflin Co., 1985), 17.

3. Fagg, *Latin America: A General History*, 165.

4. Ibid., 233.

CHAPTER FOUR: SEEKING INDEPENDENCE

1. Fagg, *Latin America: A General History*, 326.

2. Ibid., 315.

3. Ibid., 316.

4. Ibid., 327.

5. Ibid., 329.

6. Ibid., 363.

7. Ibid., 371.

CHAPTER FIVE: SELF-GOVERNMENT

1. Pierre Etienne Dostert, *Latin America: 1995, The World Today Series*, 29th ed. (Harpers Ferry, W. Virg.: Stryker-Post Publications, 1995), 41.

2. Alfred H. Kelly and Winfred A. Harbison, *The American Constitution: Its Origins and Development*, vol. 1 (New York: W.W. Norton and Co., 1948), 108–109.

3. Joseph N. Welch, *The Constitution* (Boston: Houghton Mifflin Co., 1956), 13.

4. "Brazil," *Compton's Yearbook: 1989* (F.E. Compton Co., 1989), 56.

5. Dostert, *Latin America: 1995*, 49.

6. Ibid., 71.

7. Ibid., 72.

8. Ibid., 73.

CHAPTER SIX: ALL IN THE NEIGHBORHOOD

1. Weiss, *Good Neighbors? The U.S. and Latin America*, 34.

2. "Weekend Edition, National Public Radio broadcast, March 1, 1997.

3. Dostert, *Latin America: 1995*, 77.

4. Gabriel Escobar, "Ecuadoran Lawmaker Renamed President," *The Washington Post*, Feb. 12, 1997, A26.

5. Ibid.

OTHER SOURCES

Farley Mowat, *People of the Deer* (New York, Pyramid Books, 1971).

Britannica Atlas (Chicago: Encyclopaedia Britannica, 1994).

George E. Delury, ed., *World Encyclopedia of Political Systems & Parties*, vol. 1–2 (New York: Facts on File, 1983).

People of the Ice and Snow: The American Indians (New York: Time Life Books, 1994).

William R. Shepherd, *Shepherd's Historical Atlas*, 9th edition (New York: Harper & Row, 1976).

Bliss, Michael Bliss, *Confederation 1867: The Creation of the Dominion of Canada* (New York: Franklin Watts, 1975).

FURTHER READING

Baldwin, Louis. *Intruders Within: Pueblo Resistance to Spanish Rule and the Revolt of 1680.* New York: Franklin Watts, 1995.

Bliss, Michael. *Confederation 1867: The Creation of the Dominion of Canada.* New York: Franklin Watts, 1975.

Cockcroft, James. *The Hispanic Struggle for Social Justice.* New York: Franklin Watts, 1994.

DuBois, Jill. *Cultures of the World: Colombia.* New York: Marshall Cavendish, 1991.

Feinberg, Barbara Silberdick. *Constitutional Amendments.* New York: Twenty-First Century Books, 1996.

—— . *Electing the President.* New York: Twenty-First Century Books, 1995.

Harlan, Judith. *Puerto Rico: Deciding Its Future.* New York: Twenty-First Century Books, 1996.

Humble, Richard. *The Voyages of Columbus.* New York: Franklin Watts, 1991.

——. *The Voyages of Jacques Cartier.* New York: Franklin Watts, 1993.

Kronenwetter, Michael. *Covert Action.* New York: Franklin Watts, 1991.

Law, Kevin. *Places and Peoples of the World: Canada,* New York: Chelsea House Publishers, 1990.

Macdonald, Fiona. *How Would You Survive As an Aztec?.* New York: Franklin Watts, 1995.

McIntyre, Loren. *The Incredible Incas and Their Timeless Land.* Washington, D.C.: National Geographic Society, 1975.

Malcolm, Andrew H. *The Land and People of Canada.* New York: Harper-Collins, 1991.

Pascoe, Elaine. *Mexico and the United States: Cooperation and Conflict.* New York: Twenty-First Century Books, 1996.

Vail, John J. *Fidel Castro.* New York: Chelsea House Publishers, 1988.